Tantra Kulārnava Retold
The Tantra Sect Ocean

O Beloved! Food, sleep, fear, and copulation are common to both humans and animals. But the human alone can acquire knowledge. Thus, one who is devoid of wisdom is an animal indeed. The one who is addicted to the pleasures of the world and yet boasts of the knowledge is fit to be shunned. Liberation cannot be achieved by merely smearing oneself with the ashes and by performing severe penances. What use are Vedas, Purāṇas and Āgamas if one doesn't know the true purpose of life? Wise ones keep disputing among themselves. They become bewildered by the countless scriptures and the idle talks. One should master the essence and then put the scriptures aside. The rituals and austerities are needed only until the real truth is completely realized.

INTRODUCTION

Tantra is a crucial step toward the advancement of the spiritual process and it reconciles different schools of philosophy. It seeks to harmonize the monism of Advaita with the dualism of Sānkhya and also aims to enrich knowledge with the juice of devotion. The main principle of tantra is to accept everything that is created by the divine and use every means to raise collective consciousness of the humanity. Unlike other sects, the tantra is highly rational in its approach and it asks for no faith in advance.

Lord Shiva has extracted this eternal wisdom after churning the great ocean of the Vedas, Purānas, and Āgamas. According to the Vedas, the wise cannot enjoy the pleasures of world, and one who enjoys cannot be considered the wise. But there is both enjoyment and liberation in the tantra. The knowledge of tantra can only be gained by purity of the mind and complete control over the senses.

The six main schools of the hindu philosophy are called the six limbs of tantra. The tantra scriptures are derived from the Vedas. Hence, the wise should consider Tantra as the fifth Veda. The one who follows the path of tantra without a proper guru is likely to go to hell. It is the highway to enjoyment and liberation in the highest sense. Tantra calls upon us to choose between depression and a rapid progression towards divinity. This text prescribes the modes of preparation for the highest adventure; it draws upon philosophy, religion, ethics, and yoga to elevate human life gradually to levels of the heavenly life.

Tantra acknowledges the different types of creatures based on their temperament. Then, it provides the various paths and rituals for the purification of evil instincts.

There are three types of creatures; 'Pashu' or the animal, 'Vira' or the hero, and 'Divya' or the divine. Pashu is the one who is enslaved by the eight 'Pāsha' or the shackle. The eight shackles are shame, fear, hatred, pity, ignorance, family, custom, and caste. Vira is the one who is free from the eight shackles, rejects the authority of society, and always strives for true knowledge and freedom. Divya is the one who is completely free from ego, has attained oneness with personal deity, and remains unaffected by worldly pleasures and pains. The road to absolute freedom lies in tantra, the tradition of Shakti. This is the truth and the greatest secret. This knowledge should not be disclosed to the undeserving ones.

CONTENTS

Om Mahāsoumyā Mahāghorā Kālike Namostute

Neither my mother nor my father,
Neither my family nor my friends,
Neither my husband nor my wife,
Neither my sons nor my daughters,
Neither my wealth nor my knowledge,
I depend on none except you, O Shakti!

I am filled with sin, lust, anger, and greed,
I am in the terrible ocean of birth and death,
I am a coward who dares not to face sorrow,
I am disgusted by the aimless life that I lead,
O Bhairavi! You are my refuge and only refuge.

Neither do I know practice of tantra,
Nor do I know rituals of worship,
Neither do I know art of devotion,
Nor do I know discipline of yoga,
But I know only one thing, O Tārā!
You are my refuge and only refuge.

While immersed in sorrow,
While being extremely poor,
While facing serious dangers,
While surrounded by enemies,
I always bow before you, O Kāli!
You are my one and only refuge.

CHAPTER 1
HUMAN BIRTH AND LIFE

Bhairavi, the mother of the universe, the most compassionate and merciful, asks her eternal consort Bhairava: What is the possible way by which all the creatures trapped in an endless cycle of birth and death could attain liberation?

Lord says: There's one ultimate reality; Shiva, who is attributeless, formless, all-knower, all-doer, the ruler of all, sinless, and the one without a second. Self-luminous, one without a beginning or end, without change, beyond the mind is the supreme truth. All Jiva or the embodied soul are the reflection of that supreme reality. Being attached to ignorance, regulated by egoistic tendencies and actions, they go on passing from one birth to another. Of all the births, the human birth is the most important because one becomes aware of the state of bondage and the necessity for liberation. Humans have a self-will, hence are not subject to the impulses of nature as the lower beings in the scale of evolution.

Tantra believes that human birth is obtained after going through as many as eighty-four lac lower births. Even the higher beings envy this birth because it is only during human life that change, progress and finally liberation are possible. Purānas declare that the very deities have to come down and take a body if they wish to advance on the ladder of cosmic existence.

The value of the human body is not fully realized by everyone. The pleasures of the senses can be gained easily but not so a human birth with a sound body. One who is so endowed with a noble birth and yet fails to use it for one's upliftment is indeed a self-slayer.

The human body is meant to be protected and nourished to achieve the highest goal called 'Moksha' or the liberation. Therefore, the desire for self-preservation exists in everyone despite unbearable pain and suffering.

One must protect oneself as to live according to 'Dharma' or the righteousness. Dharma leads to wisdom, which leads to the state of meditation and inevitably to liberation. Therefore, one must protect this human body to realize the supreme truth.

If you don't work out the means for your liberation now, when else will it be possible? It will never be possible. The condition in which you live now pursues you everywhere. It is vain to expect that things will improve after the death. The state of consciousness attained while living in the body is the same consciousness after you leave the body. As here so there. The world you reach after death is determined by your current level of consciousness. So, as long as the body lasts, strive tirelessly towards the goal of moksha.

Remember, the body does not last forever. The age diminishes like the water in a broken pot and the diseases strike like an enemy. Before the adversities dawn upon you, come to the right path. In worldly pursuits, the time flies unnoticed. Youth is like a dream and life is momentary like lightning. Even a hundred years is too little; for half the life is spent in sleep and the other half is made unproductive by infancy, disease, suffering, and oldness. Need not sleep when you are supposed to be awake. Deluded by ignorance, one looks not at what one sees, listens not at what one hears, and follows not what one understands. One fails to realize that each moment this body is decaying. Death swallows one when still thinking of what is not done and what is yet to be done. Therefore, complete today without fail what is to be done by tomorrow.

Helplessly, one swing from birth to death and again from death to birth. Freedom from the desires is the only way to reach liberation. Therefore, give up the attachments fully, not just by the mind, but by the whole of your being. If you cannot do it due to weakness, then resort to the company of saints. The holy company acts as a medicine. One who has no company of holy, no discrimination, and no purity is indeed blind. How can such a person fail to take the wrong path? Engaged constantly in the pleasures of food, wine, sleep, and sex, one is no more than an animal. Humans should pursue the real goal in life of acquiring the knowledge of the supreme truth.

Engaged ceaselessly in the performance of worldly duties, humans fail to seek a higher purpose. Engrossed in rituals and austerities, they fail to realize their true self. They are deluded by the elaborate sacrifices. How could anyone achieve freedom by punishing the body? Beware of fake gurus, who are intent on amassing wealth, attired in disguise, they wander everywhere as wise and throw others in delusion. Attached to the pleasures of the world, they proclaim, 'I know the supreme truth'. They are fit to be shunned completely. The animals wander about naked without shame and live in the mud and ashes. Thus, do they become yogi? Frogs and fishes live all their lives in the holy river. Do they acquire special merit? Truly, such self-denials are only for deceiving the world.

The only means for liberation is the divine knowledge. This truth is not known to those who are engaged constantly in debates about the six philosophies or caught up in the subtleties of scriptures. They turn their backs on the real truth to protect their ego and wander over countless books ceaselessly. They study the Vedas and yet fight among themselves. Forgetting that the truth is within, they look for it outside.

The one whose intelligence is awakened can only benefit from the authentic scriptures. Others study the scriptures to fool themselves. Endless are scriptures, but the lifespan is limited. Hence, it needs pure wisdom to go straight to the essence of scriptures, like a swan sipping milk out of water. Study the scriptures to know the essence and then leave them aside, just like you leave husk after collecting the grains out of it.

Once the supreme truth is realized, all other knowledge is useless. Liberation is not achieved by chanting the Vedas or by studying the scriptures. Neither the prescribed stages in life, nor philosophies, nor sciences can give true liberation. The divine knowledge can only lead to liberation and this knowledge should be received through the mouth of a real guru. All other ways are deceptive. Remember, true knowledge alone is life-giving.

The supreme knowledge declared by the Lord is always free from rituals and austerities. It should be received through the mouth of a guru. Shiva only speaks through the guru to the disciple. One is certainly delivered from the bonds of the world after receiving such knowledge. Wisdom is of two kinds: the knowledge derived from scriptures and knowledge born of mental reasoning. Some prefer dualism while others prefer non-dualism. But none of them knows the real truth, which is beyond both dualism and non-dualism.

'I', 'Me', and 'Mine' are the terms responsible for the bondage. The wise detaches oneself from such terms and always strives for liberation. The true action and the true knowledge are that which frees; all other action gives only fatigue, and all other knowledge gives only headache.

Think not of the higher purpose as long as there is activity of the senses, agitation of the thoughts and the mind is not steady. Talk of it not as long as you are identified with the body and the real guru has no grace. The restraints, observances, austerities, pilgrimage, scriptures, and worship are needed only as long as the supreme truth is not realized.

Always be mindful of the supreme truth, and remain dedicated to it in any situation with full effort. As you are suffering, take refuge under the divine tree of liberation, on whose branches the flower of dharma and wisdom grows, and whose fruit is the ultimate bliss.

CHAPTER 2
THE GLORY OF TANTRA

So, what is Tantra?

Handed down from mouth to mouth in the long stretch of holy tradition, the doctrine of tantra is the highest truth, which is well guarded from the unqualified and undeserving ones. There are a total of eight paths for liberation in the tantra.

The first is the Veda path, where the actions are considered most important. The second, higher than the Veda is the Vaishnava path, where devotion to the Lord plays a greater role than actions itself. The third, higher than Vaishnava is the Shaiva path, where wisdom and meditation play a greater role than anything else. The fourth, higher than Shaiva is the Shākta path, where complete surrender is practiced in a real sense. The first four paths are meant for a seeker without much control over the senses called Pashu.

The fifth is Dakshina path, where action, devotion, and knowledge are harmonized; the fruits of the first four paths are organized and conserved here. The sixth, higher than Dakshina is the Vāma path, where everything in creation is used as a means for returning to the one base consciousness. The Dakshina and Vāma paths are meant for an evolved seeker called Vira, who can struggle against forces of darkness to reach the divine within.

The seventh is Aghora path, where worldly and spiritual pleasures are finally harmonized. The fruits of the Dakshina and Vāma paths are organized and conserved here.

The eighth, higher than Aghora is the Kaula path, where the things are finally seen as they are in reality. The Aghora and Kaula paths are meant for the highest type of seeker called Divya.

The highest of all the doctrines is Kaula, the most secret path. There is nothing higher than this, which is the essence of all essences, which has been passed down through guru shishya tradition from time immemorial. As the footprints of small animals get lost in the footprint of an elephant, so do different philosophies get absorbed in this doctrine. All other paths finally merge into this path only.

In the Kaula path, what is normally called sin and evil is turned into a force of virtue, the very pleasures of the world become a means for the liberation. Even the gods of the higher realms like Brahmā, Vishnu, and Rudra follow this path of harmony, what to speak of an ordinary human. So, if you aspire for fulfillment, then give up all other philosophies, all other ways, and come to the tantra.

Beware, the tantra is not for everyone. There are certain conditions to be satisfied before the knowledge of tantra can be revealed. One must have a mature mind and a good intention as a result of the disciplines undergone in the past births. There must be complete faith in the personal deity, the guru, and above all, the divine grace should be there. It cannot be attained by the undeserving ones nor does it stay with them.

The guru should first initiate the disciples and prepare them, then reveal the highest knowledge. Without any elaborate rituals and austerities, the tantra is capable of leading to the final liberation. Even if you lack the full knowledge of the tradition, only faith and dedication are enough to deliver liberation.

The one whose faith remains unshakable even amid the unbearable suffering is verily praised by the deities. The one who follows this path becomes one with the Shiva itself. The one who is constantly afflicted by diseases, poverty, and misery; yet keeps an unshakable faith in the divine mother attains to the highest state of liberation. The tantra should not be forsaken whatever your state, whether you receive praise or blame, whether you become rich or poor, and whether you die today or at the end of your age.

Surviving is not a big deal; animals, birds, and trees are all living. The one whose mind is always fixed on dharma only truly lives. The days come and go without meaning for the one who is not following the path of dharma.

Who then is a true Tāntrika?

Bestowed with the grace of the guru, devoid of the evil ways by the means of initiation, and delighting in the worship of divine mother, one becomes a true tāntrika. In such a fortunate one only the wisdom of tantra takes root and grows without much effort.

True tāntrika are Shākta from the within but appear as Shaiva from the outside. When among the people in the society, they act as a Vaishnava. The glory of the tantra is known only to those who are sincerely devoted to the divine mother. Hence, the tantra knowledge must be protected from the undeserving ones at any cost.

The world is made up of Shiva and Shakti i.e. consciousness and energy. Tantra is based on the truth of both and therefore it is the most accurate science and complete in itself. The six philosophies say the Lord, is my six limbs, and one who differentiates among them cuts my body.

The scriptures of the Tantra contain the knowledge of the Vedas. The tantra need not prove its excellence, since it comes directly from the mouth of Shiva. The immediate benefits are a sufficient justification for its claim to be the highest scripture. It is open to all to verify its claim. The one which gives immediate results and direct realization should be considered as the highest teaching.

Those who have created strong bonds of sins in past births don't gain the grace of the guru. A sinner, even though knowing the path of tantra doesn't turn to it; but one who has accumulated merits in the past crores of births comes to tantra even though prevented from it. This is the means revealed by the divine mother for the attainment of both enjoyment and liberation. It is impossible to understand the tantra fully unless favored by the grace of the guru and the divine mother.

If by mere drinking of the wine, one was to attain fulfillment, all drunkards would reach perfection. If by merely eating the meat, one was to achieve the highest state, all meat-eaters in the world would become liberated. if by mere copulation all creatures could attain eternal bliss, then there would be no suffering in the world. Tantra is not to be shunned, but those fools who follow their instincts without understanding the way laid down by the tradition and the tantric scriptures. It is vain to drink alcohol, rather it is a sin. Similarly, eating meat for one's enjoyment is the greatest sin. But, when the prohibited items are purified through proper rituals and the partaker reaches certain state of consciousness, then those items lead to merit.

The sure means for liberation is preserved in the tantra, preached by none other than Shiva. Rules declared in the scriptures are to be followed blindly until the state of true wisdom is achieved.

CHAPTER 3
LORD SHIVA FIVE FACES

Lord is eternal and the supreme truth, who has disclosed the dharma in various ways to suit the different times. Lord through five faces, having different powers, preached the five ways to liberation.

Shiva preached the path of mantra through the East face, which has the power of creation, and whose principles are twenty-four. Lord preached the path of devotion through the South face, which has the power of sustenance, and whose principles are twenty-five. Lord preached the path of action facing the West having the power of destruction, whose principles are thirty-two. Facing the North having the power of compassion, the Lord preached the path of knowledge, whose principles are thirty-six. Facing upward having the power of secrecy, the Lord preached the highest truth, whose principle is the 'Brahma' itself.

Each way has its own mantras and the sub-mantras leading to both enjoyment and liberation. The fruit of each mantra is granted by the deity presiding over that mantra. And all the deities are nothing but portions of the Lord Shiva and Mother Shakti. The truth of all the mantras is known to the Lord alone and out of the divine grace that humans come to know of it.

Any one of the four faces is enough for liberation. And if one were to know all four faces of the Lord, then one would become Shiva itself. But higher than all the four faces put together is the upper face, which is the essence of dharma because it can be practiced only in a higher state of consciousness. It is the most direct means for liberation, yielding greater fruit than all other ways.

Obtaining the full knowledge of the upper face from the mouth of a guru, you will attain liberation in this very life, and also gain prosperity and power. The knowledge preached through the upper face of the Lord is to be cherished above all other ways.

The greatest mantra presiding over the upper face of the Lord is 'Soham'. The 'So' stands for Shakti i.e. creation and birth, whereas the 'Ham' for Shiva i.e. destruction and death. Both together make creation possible. They are present in every form, whether living or non-living. Each inhalation chants 'So' and each exhalation chants 'Ham'. Thus, the whole existence is repeating this mantra constantly. The mantra 'Soham' is composed of the two Sanskrit words; 'Saḥ' which means 'That' and 'Aham' which means 'I'. Hence, the mantra means 'I Am That'. As a big tree resides inside a small seed, the whole creation resides in this great mantra. By constantly repeating this mantra, even a pashu can become the pashupati. The seer of this mantra is Sadā Shiva, the meter is Gāyatri, and the presiding deity is Ādi Shakti. One who masters this mantra realizes the supreme truth.

There is no one higher than Guru, no god greater than Shiva, no science better than Vedas, no philosophy clearer than Tantra, no happiness gratifying than Wisdom, no fruit tastier than Liberation. This is the truth, the sole truth.

CHAPTER 4
THE FIVE MAKĀRA RITUAL

The ingredients to be used in the worship of the divine mother are of different kinds. In tantra, we use five items starting with the letter 'M' well known as 'Panchamakāra'. They are 'Madya' or the wine, 'Mānsa' or the meat, 'Matsya' or the fish, 'Mudrā' or the money, and 'Maithuna' or the copulation. The scriptures describe in great detail the various types of vessels to be used on different occasions and their dimensions; the several types of grains to be used, the proportion of their mixing and the manner of cooking; and the preparation of various kinds of wine from the different substances.

The wine is primarily used as a tool for curbing the senses from straying over external objects. It is used as an agent for the purification of the mind and the consciousness. In its fragrance is activated the power of will, in its taste is awakened the power of knowledge, in its absorption the power of action, and its drinking the supreme state is achieved.

There are several types of meat described in the tantric scriptures. But it was made clear that meat is to be used only for the ritualistic purpose. No creature shall be harmed for one's enjoyment. Not even a blade of grass must be cut without a valid purpose. What is called sin becomes a merit, if it is done for a higher purpose. When used properly, the means of fall becomes the means for liberation.

When the ingredients are consecrated and offered with devotion, then the devotee's heart becomes filled with supreme bliss. This ultimate bliss experienced within cannot be disturbed by anything.

In this condition, it seems as if one were possessed by the deity, Bhairava or Bhairavi. The true self veiled by ignorance is released for some time. Not intoxication, but a withdrawal from the external stress and anxiety leads to a relaxed state of consciousness. This is the immediate effect of the correct wine ritual.

No one is allowed to take part in the ritual as a mere creature. The wine is the Shiva and the meat or fish is the Shakti, and one who partakes is none other than the Bhairava or Bhairavi, the divine enjoyer. The bliss that arises when both the items are fused in the consciousness of the practitioner is liberation in a real sense. Bliss is the true nature of the soul, and the wine brings it out. This is the reason why yogi takes the sanctified wine.

There are conditions to be fulfilled before one is allowed to drink wine. One must be free from all doubts, brave of the heart, above all dualities, above curiosity, and have a thorough understanding of tantra. Wine should be taken only as long as the mind is not shaken and the sight is not affected. In such a person alone the partaking of wine sanctified by the mantras, awakens the sense of divineness.

The deity must be worshipped according to the rituals prescribed in the scriptures. Offer to the guru before partaking of the wine and the meat. Wine is to be taken only for the concentration of the mind and steadying contemplation on the divine. One sin who drinks the wine just for pleasure.

There are restrictions to be followed before one is allowed to earn money. One must be fully free from greed, above pleasure seeking, devoid of possessiveness, and always ready to donate it for a good purpose. The money can be earned as long as there is no greed or fear arising out of it.

One should earn money only to take care of the basic needs i.e. food, clothing, shelter, and thereon resort to the higher purpose. One sin who earns just to fulfill own selfish desires.

There are some rules to be followed before one becomes eligible for copulation. One must be completely free from the lust, above the individual ego, above shame and fear, devoid of anger, and fully devoted to the divine mother. One who copulates for the sake of pleasure certainly goes to the hell. All males are the incarnation of Bhairava and all females are Bhairavi. Both unite to make the life possible. After knowing everything about copulation from a guru, you will become one with the divine in this very life.

One who is overcome by intoxication is aware of nothing; for that person, there is no dharma, no meditation, no worship, no virtue, no austerity, and no guru. One may be most learned in the sciences and the scriptures, but if that person drinks wine, eats meat, and copulates with women just for one's enjoyment. Then, that one is indeed blameworthy.

In Tantra, the practitioners are divided into three broad categories; Pashu, Vira, and Divya. Five ingredients have different meanings for each class of seeker; the symbolic meaning for Divya, the literal meaning for Vira, and the substitutional meaning for Pashu. The divya people use the wine of divine intoxication, the meat of silence, the fish of breath control, the money of concentration, and the copulation of one's ego with the divine. For the pashu people, there is a substitution for each item. The coconut water or milk for wine, the ginger or garlic for meat, the brinjal or radish for fish, the rice or wheat for money, and the meditation upon the lotus feet of the divine mother for copulation.

CHAPTER 5
THE RULES OF WORSHIP

Everyone is not eligible for the worship of a deity. To summon a deity and make offerings requires a preparation, external and internal, worked out in the present life or past lives. One who is so competent is fully initiated and knows the real truth. One who is full of devotion for the guru as well as for the personal deity having full control over senses, and is well disciplined in life is considered initiated in a real sense. The mysteries of the Āgamas, which are not all openly discussed in the scriptures, are known to that person. Worship should not be done as a mere routine or as a part of the daily mundane activity. One who truly worships looks forward to it with utmost eagerness being pure of heart, superbly joyous, devoid of anger and agitation, rejecting the inferior rituals, and cheerful of continence. True devotion doesn't come in a day. Even when it is intense, it does not last long. The lasting devotion sprouts after a long period of intense worship and by the grace of the divine mother. It is then that offerings made according to the instructions of the guru reach the destination. It is then that the worship of the great Shri Chakra, the abode of the divine mother, can be performed correctly using the mantra yoga. When devotee enters into worship, one must be in a divine state of consciousness. To truly commune with the divine, one must be aware of one's divinity. Such a worshipper attains enjoyment as well as liberation without much effort.

Worship must be performed in such a place that is free from all distractions and disturbances, and also free from the crowd. The worshipper should be seated in a comfortable position which gives stability to the body, and face either the east or north direction.

Before starting the ritual, one should visualize oneself seated in the blissful abode of the divine mother in the ocean of immortality with all the ingredients required for 'Puja' or the worship and perform it according to the orders of the guru. The fivefold purification should be done before proceeding to the puja. The purification of oneself, the place, the materials used, the mantras, and the deity idol.

The purification of oneself; both outer and inner. The outer by bath and inner by purification of the five elements using breath control and other prescribed methods. The place of worship is sanctified by cleaning and wiping, also decorating it with flowers, incense, camphor, and the colorful lights. The substances used for worship should be purified by sprinkling it with the sanctified water while reciting the mantras. The great mantras should be unlocked by the appropriate means to make it fruitful. Lastly, the deity idol should be purified by placing it on a high seat, then invoking energy of the deity into it while sprinkling with the sanctified water in prescribed manner, also adorning it with the ornaments while offering incense and lights afterward.

After the comprehensive purification process, attention should be paid to the drawing of sacred geometries called the 'Mandala', the proper placement and utilization of various shapes, singly and in combination; the various cosmic powers are invoked through the prescribed mantras that are repeated in a proper order. The gurus should be meditated upon. And after sanctifying the seat, the deity is summoned. The whole process of worship should be done with an exclusive concentration.

The divine is certainly formless and attributeless. How is it possible that it's worshipped in so many different forms and its attributes are explained in countless scriptures? Āgamas give answers to this.

The divine is indeed the unknowable, formless, attributeless, and pure consciousness. Yet for the benefit of devotees, it takes diverse forms. Thus, the supreme deity should not be limited to any form. It reveals itself in the various forms. The worshipper visualizes the formless in the form and adores the divine in the symbols like sky, air, fire, water, and mandala.

The cream as long as remains hidden in the milk does not nourish anyone. But when it is collected and treated properly; it promotes nourishment. The divine is present everywhere but without proper evocation and the methods of worship, it does not yield fruit.

All the energies of the deity should be summoned together in an idol, and then the living deity should be worshipped. Otherwise, the worship is considered fruitless. There might be defects in the process, mantra, or the rituals; still if the summon of deity is done correctly, then the worship bears fruit.

Only when the rituals are performed according to the rules laid down by the authentic scriptures that it become acceptable to the deity. If worship is offered without an awareness that the divine is pervading in the form of the mantra, then it is useless indeed. 'Yantra' or the instrument is declared to be embodied by mantra. Worshipped in the form of yantra, the divine mother is very easily pleased. Why is it called Yantra? Because it subdues and regulates all misery arising from desire, anger, and greed. As the body is to the soul, so is the yantra to the deity. The deity should be carefully summoned inside a yantra and worshipped with all requirements. Each deity should be invoked with proper honor and grace. Thus, know everything about the yantra from the mouth of a guru and worship according to the rules.

CHAPTER 6
THE PATH OF YOGA

Yoga is a process of union between Shakti and Shiva. Tantra seeks to weave it into our everyday life by giving a different meaning to each of the activities. Thus, yoga is a means for progression from an ordinary human to the divine.

'Dhyana' or the meditation is an important part of yoga. it is of two types; gross and subtle. When the meditation is done using a form, it is called gross; when it is done without a form, it is called subtle. Gross meditation is used when the mind is very unsteady and needs a support, a concrete object on which to fix itself so that it becomes unwavering. But the aim of both types of meditation is the same, steadiness of the mind.

When the divine is imagined with a form, it is contemplated with a body having several heads and limbs. Whereas when it is imagined without a form, it is contemplated as the existence, consciousness, and bliss, who is shining without a body. It neither rises nor sets, neither waxes nor wanes, it shines by itself and illuminates others without effort. It is infinite, and is formed of light not seen through the eyes, but can only be felt by the heart.

One whose movement of breath is arrested, who is immobile like a stone, and fixed on the supreme self is called a yogi, the knower of yoga. Where there is no awareness, devoid of movement, and a state of complete stillness; that meditation devoid of any form is called 'Samādhi' or the absorption. In this state, the truth shines by itself without any mental thinking.

One who seems as if asleep while waking, neither inhaling nor exhaling and immobile, is truly freed. One whose senses are without agitation, whose mind and breath are absorbed in oneself, who is like the dead, is called the liberated while living. That one neither sees nor hears nor smells nor touches nor tastes, neither knows pleasure nor pain, neither exercises the mind nor thinks. Like a log of wood, one is aware of nothing; one is completely absorbed in the divine consciousness. When the water is mixed with milk no difference remains, similarly no difference remains between Jiva and the divine. An ordinary human becomes divine in the state of samādhi. Once the true self is detached from three gunas, it never falls into the world again; just as cream extracted from milk never dissolves into it again.

The one who comes to know the supreme reality beyond the forms and above all the changes, the very mantras become servants. One who is established in the supreme consciousness, for that person each movement is a worship, each word is a mantra, and each gaze is meditation. When the identification with the body is completely discarded, then the true self is realized. After that, wherever the mind goes, it remains firmly established in the samādhi.

Yoga is the union of a soul with the divine, so declare the wise by the authority of the authentic scriptures. When the supreme self is realized, all doubts and karma are washed away. One cares not for the status of the gods or mighty demons when the yogi attains the supreme state. The one who experiences the all-pervading, blissful, and imperishable self, for that yogi what can remain to be attained or known in this world? When the state of eternal bliss is achieved, neither breath control nor meditation is compulsory. Enough of the restraints and observances once the supreme self is realized.

When the supreme self is meditated upon even for a moment with faith, the immeasurable is the fruit. Even reflection is done for a moment on the truth that 'I Am That' wipes out all sins as the sun dispels all darkness. The knower of the truth reaps a millionfold fruit than those who practice the restraints, observances, sacrifices, pilgrimages, and donations.

There are several states of consciousness in the life of a yogi. The highest is the natural state in which oneness with the divine is always felt simply; the lower is concentration and meditation; the still lower is chanting and studying scriptures; and the lowest is worship and sacrifice.

A billion worship equals a hymn, a billion hymn equals a chanting, a billion chanting equals a meditation, and a billion meditation equals a samādhi.

Free from the rituals is the highest worship; silence is the highest chanting; absence of thoughts is the highest meditation; and the absence of desire is the highest samādhi. The yogi should always perform the worship without any rituals and mantras. Free from attachments, beyond all desires and associations, always absorbed in the supreme self, the yogi knows the real truth.

The body itself is the temple. Jiva itself is the divine. Remove the veil of ignorance from the mind and worship with the awareness of 'Soham' or 'I Am That'. Enclosed in husk, it is called paddy; freed from husk, it is called rice. Enslaved in body, it is called Jiva; freed from body, it is called Shiva.

To the wise, the divine reveals itself in the sacrificial fire; to the thinker in the mind; to the devotee in the heart; to the ignorant in the idols or the images; but for those who know the supreme truth, the divine is pervading everywhere.

One who remains calm in either praise or blame, always devoid of either exuberance or depression in any situation is truly a yogi. The knower of the supreme truth dwells in the body like a vagabond, devoid of desire, ever fearless, master of the senses, and free from choices. The yogi lives like the stupid, dull, blind, deaf, impotent, and intoxicated.

Yogis can dwell anywhere, disguised in any form, unknown to all. They are intent on the welfare of all, and thus stand unnoticed. They do not show their self-knowledge at once. Among people, they live as dull and intoxicated. The yogi is not easily perceived, like stars in the presence of the sun. The adepts in the yoga appear lowly, speak in a vulgar manner, and behave as if ignorant. They do so to avoid needless attention. They live in such a way that the world may laugh, feel disgusted, and leave them alone. The yogi who has become one in the heart with the divine remains untainted by all actions. Ever desireless, the yogi lives out of compassion for all the creatures.